SWAMP THINGS
Animal Life in a Wetland

Muskrat

by Ellen Lawrence

Consultant:

Adam A. Ahlers, Assistant Professor
Department of Horticulture and Natural Resources
Kansas State University
Manhattan, Kansas

BEARPORT
PUBLISHING

New York, New York

Credits

Cover, © tbkmedia.de/Alamy; 4T, © TRIG/Shutterstock; 4B, © Roger de Montfort/Shutterstock; 5, © Michael C. Gray/Shutterstock; 7, © Joseph Scott Photography/Shutterstock; 8, © Brian Lasenby/Shutterstock; 9, © Andril Myronov/Shutterstock; 10, © Public Domain; 11, © Sergey Uryadnikov/Shutterstock; 12T, © Artur Synenko/Shutterstock; 12B, © Tom Reichner/Shutterstock; 13, © Jussi Murtosaari/Nature Picture Library; 14, © S. R. Maglione/Shutterstock; 15L, © David Havel/Shutterstock; 15R, © Michael Quinton/Minden Pictures/FLPA; 16, © John Cancalosi/Alamy; 17, © NHPA/Superstock; 18T, © Vincent Vicari; 18B, © John Beatty/Open.tours Immersive Media; 19, © Tony Cambell/Shutterstock; 20, © Eduard Kyslynskyy/Shutterstock; 21, © Braud, Dominique/Animals Animals; 22TR, © Sandra Slaymaker; 22BL, © Jonah Evans/www.naturetracking.com; 22BR, © blickwinkel/Alamy; 23TL, © Lars-Ove Jonsson/Shutterstock; 23TC, © NHPA/Superstock; 23TR, © Tony Moran/Shutterstock; 23BL, © John Cancalosi/Alamy; 23BC, © Menno Schaefer/Shutterstock; 23BR, © Martha Marks/Shutterstock.

Publisher: Kenn Goin
Editor: Jessica Rudolph
Creative Director: Spencer Brinker
Design: Emma Randall
Photo Researcher: Ruby Tuesday Books Ltd

Library of Congress Cataloging-in-Publication Data

Names: Lawrence, Ellen, 1967– , author.
Title: Muskrat / by Ellen Lawrence.
Description: New York, New York : Bearport Publishing, 2017. | Series: Swamp
   things : animal life in a wetland | Includes bibliographical references
   and index. | Audience: Ages 5 to 8.
Identifiers: LCCN 2016023111 (print) | LCCN 2016024915 (ebook) | ISBN
   9781944102555 (library) | ISBN 9781944997199 (Ebook)
Subjects: LCSH: Muskrat—Juvenile literature.
Classification: LCC QL737.R666 L39 2017 (print) | LCC QL737.R666 (ebook) |
   DDC 599.35—dc23
LC record available at https://lccn.loc.gov/2016023111

For more information, write to Bearport Publishing Company, Inc., 45 West 21st Street, Suite 3B, New York, New York 10010. Printed in the United States of America.

10 9 8 7 6 5 4 3 2 1

Contents

Meet a Muskrat

It's a warm afternoon in the Atchafalaya (*uh*-chaf-uh-LYE-uh) Swamp.

On the edge of a shallow pond, cattail plants sway in the breeze.

A furry brown muskrat gnaws through the plants.

Once the little animal has cut down several cattails, it picks them up in its mouth.

Then it swims across the pond to find a safe place to eat.

cattail plants

a muskrat chewing on a plant

4

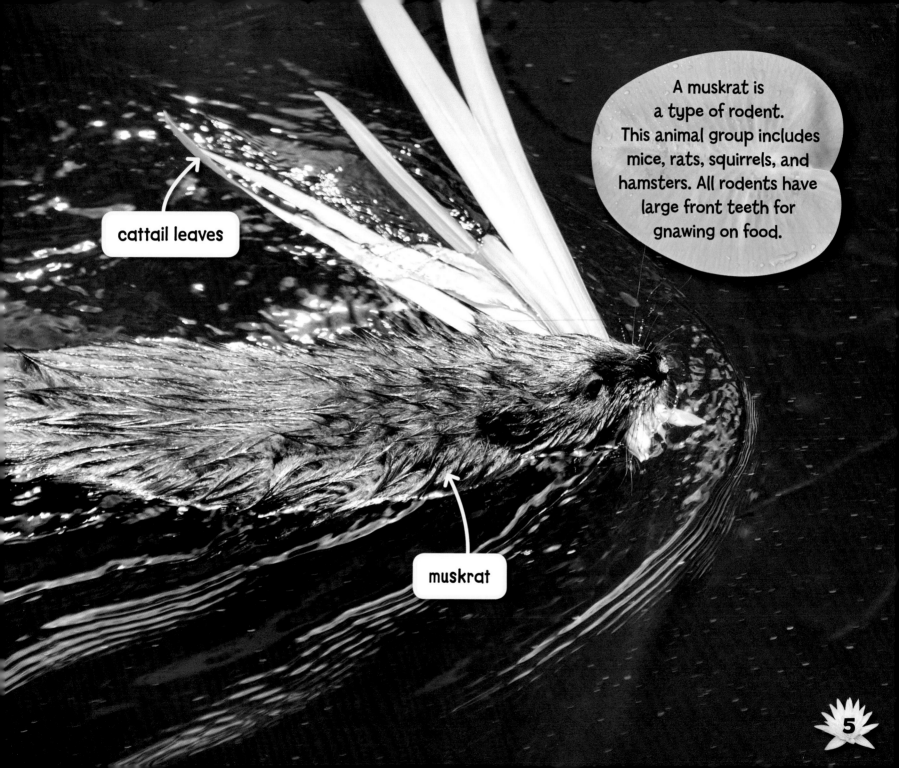

A Wet World

Muskrats make their homes in watery places such as **wetlands**.

In some places in a wetland, cattails, tough grasses, and other plants grow from the wet ground.

In other areas, known as swamps, trees and bushes grow from the water-covered land.

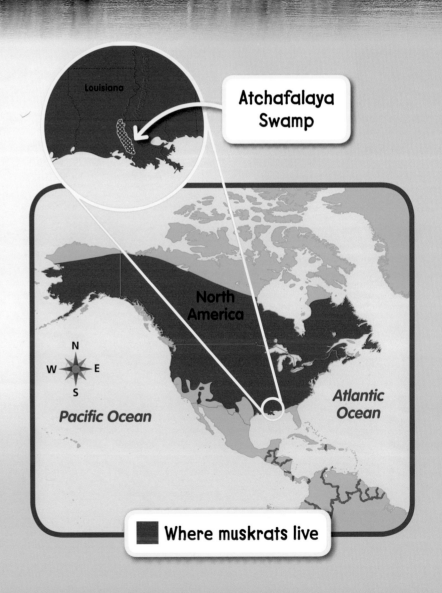

Atchafalaya Swamp

Louisiana

North America

Pacific Ocean

Atlantic Ocean

■ Where muskrats live

A muskrat gets
its name because it
looks like a large rat.
It also gives off a strong
scent known as musk.

All About Muskrats

A muskrat has a round body covered in thick, brown fur.

Its black tail is almost hairless.

A muskrat's large back feet help it paddle through the water.

The animal also has long claws for digging in mud.

Why do you think muskrats dig in the mud?

claws

An adult muskrat is about 22 inches (56 cm) long from its nose to the end of its tail. It can weigh up to 4 pounds (1.8 kg).

Busy Builders

Muskrats build homes called **lodges** in shallow ponds and lakes.

To make a lodge, a muskrat piles up mud, plant stems, and leaves.

Inside the dome-shaped heap, the animal builds a room for sleeping.

Using its claws, a muskrat also digs homes called **dens** in the muddy banks of rivers, ponds, and lakes.

muskrat lodge

Muskrats also build raft-like structures that float in the water. What do you think they use these for?

Munching Muskrats

When it's not building homes, a muskrat spends a lot of time eating.

It searches for food in the water close to its den or lodge.

It eats water plants such as cattails, water lilies, pondweed, and ferns.

In winter, however, there are fewer plants to feed on.

Then the animal hunts for crayfish, snails, frogs, and fish.

water lily

frog

How do you think a muskrat stays safe from animals that want to eat it?

A muskrat uses mud and plants to build a platform that floats in the water. It carries food to the platform, then climbs on board to safely eat its meal.

feeding platform

13

Dangerous Neighbors

Muskrats share their wetland homes with many dangerous **predators**.

Minks, otters, bobcats, and foxes eat muskrats.

Owls, hawks, and large snakes also hunt the little creatures.

If a predator comes close, a muskrat will dive under the water to escape.

Muskrats are strong swimmers, and they can hold their breath for more than ten minutes.

owl

dead muskrat

fox

bobcat

muskrat

If a muskrat can't escape to the water in time, it will bite and scratch an attacker to try to save itself.

Muskrat Moms

In early spring, male and female muskrats meet up and **mate**.

About 30 days after mating, the female gives birth inside a den or lodge.

The tiny babies are called kits.

They cannot see and they have no fur.

a pair of muskrats on top of a lodge

Mini Muskrats

For the first few weeks, muskrat kits stay inside their home.

They sleep and drink milk from their mother's body.

By the time they are one month old, the kits have fur and they can see.

Now, when their mom leaves the family's home, the kits go with her.

The little muskrats explore and search for plants to eat.

kits napping outside the den

a one-month-old kit

18

Growing Up in a Wetland

Once the kits are six weeks old, they are ready to live on their own.

The kits' parents mate again.

In a single year, a pair of muskrats may have three litters of kits.

After leaving their parents, young muskrats begin building their own homes in their watery world!

male muskrats fighting

Male muskrats are fierce fighters. They often fight each other over food or the best places to build homes.

Use these words to describe how
a muskrat builds its homes:

gnaws   plants   claws   digs   mud

21

Science Lab

Be a Muskrat Scientist

Imagine you are a scientist who studies muskrats. You must look for clues that muskrats are living in a wetland area.

Look carefully at the three photos. Each one contains a clue.

What do you think each of the photos shows? Write your ideas in your notebook.

(The answers are on page 24.)

Science Words

dens (DENZ) homes, often dug underground, where animals can rest, be safe, and have babies

litter (LIT-ur) a group of animals that are born to the same mother at the same time

lodges (LAHJ-ihz) homes built by an animal from mud and plants, usually near or in water

mate (MAYT) to come together to produce young

predators (PRED-uh-turz) animals that hunt and kill other animals for food

wetlands (WET-landz) habitats where most of the land is covered with shallow water and plants

23

Index

Read More

Owen, Ruth. *Welcome to the Pond (Nature's Neighborhoods: All About Ecosystems).* New York: Ruby Tuesday Books (2016).

Reingold, Adam. *The Beaver's Lodge: Building with Leftovers (Spectacular Animal Towns).* New York: Bearport (2010).

Silverman, Buffy. *Wetlands (Habitat Survival).* Chicago: Heinemann-Raintree (2013).

Learn More Online

To learn more about muskrats, visit **www.bearportpublishing.com/SwampThings**

About the Author

Ellen Lawrence lives in the United Kingdom. Her favorite books to write are those about nature and animals. In fact, the first book Ellen bought for herself, when she was six years old, was the story of a gorilla named Patty Cake that was born in New York's Central Park Zoo.

Answers for Page 22

Picture A shows muskrat footprints in mud.
Picture B shows muskrat poop.
Picture C shows the entrance to a muskrat den.